Spiralizer Recipes

Spiralizer Cookbook with Keto & Paleo Friendly, Low-Carb, and Delicious Meat & Fish Spiralized Recipes for a Healthy Lifestyle

(Spiralize Everything Book 4)

Copyright © 2019 Brendan Fawn
All rights reserved.
ISBN: 9781080315413

Text Copyright © [Brendan Fawn]
All rights reserved. No part of this guide may be reproduced in any form without permission in writing from the publisher except in the case of brief quotations embodied in critical articles or reviews.

Legal & Disclaimer
The information contained in this book and its contents is not designed to replace or take the place of any form of medical or professional advice; and is not meant to replace the need for independent medical, financial, legal or other professional advice or services, as may be required. The content and information in this book has been provided for educational and entertainment purposes only.

The content and information contained in this book has been compiled from sources deemed reliable, and it is accurate to the best of the Author's knowledge, information, and belief. However, the Author cannot guarantee its accuracy and validity and cannot be held liable for any errors and/or omissions. Further, changes are periodically made to this book as and when needed. Where appropriate and/or necessary, you must consult a professional (including but not limited to your doctor, attorney, financial advisor or such other professional advisor) before using any of the suggested remedies, techniques, or information in this book.

Upon using the contents and information contained in this book, you agree to hold harmless the Author from and against any damages, costs, and expenses, including any legal fees potentially resulting from the application of any of the information provided by this book. This disclaimer applies to any loss, damages or injury caused by the use and application, whether directly or indirectly, of any advice or information presented, whether for breach of contract, tort, negligence, personal injury, criminal intent, or under any other cause of action.

You agree to accept all risks of using the information presented in this book.

Table of Contents

Introduction 6

Kitchen Utensils That You Will Need to Prepare Spiralizer Recipes 8

Spiralized Meat & Fish Dishes 11

Spiralized Carrots with Shrimps, Pineapple and Raisins 11

Spiralized Zucchini with Shrimps, Pineapple and Apricots 14

Spiralized Potatoes with Shrimps, Pineapple and Celery 17

Spiralized Squash with Shrimps, Carrots and Plums 20

Spiralized Cabbage with Shrimps, Onions and Plums 22

Inspiralized Carrots with Beef, Milk and Walnuts 24

Inspiralized Zucchini with Beef, Milk and Peanuts 26

Spiralized Potatoes with Beef, Beer and Walnuts 29

Spiralized Squash with Pork, Beer and Peanuts 31

Spiralized Cabbage with Pork, Beer and Peanuts 33

Spiralized Cabbage with Turkey and Cashews 36

Spiralized Potatoes with Turkey and Zucchini 38

Spiralized Potatoes with Chicken and Carrots 41

Inspiralized Onions with Lamb and Mayonnaise 43

Inspiralized Onions with Lamb and Wine 45

Salmon in Mayonnaise and Spiralized Zucchini 47

Tuna in Garlic Mayonnaise with Peanuts and Spiralized Zucchini 50

Garlic Tuna and Spiralized Squash 53

Tuna in Garlic Mayonnaise with Walnuts and Spiralized Zucchini 56

Hake in Garlic Mayonnaise with Peanuts and Spiralized Carrots 59

Grilled Lamb in Garlic Mayonnaise with Spiralized Zucchini and Celery 61

Grilled Shrimps with Spiralized Zucchini (Cover Recipe) 64

Grilled Shrimps with Oranges and Spiralized Pineapple 66

Grilled Chicken with Oranges and Spiralized Pineapple 68

Grilled Pork in Mayonnaise with Spiralized Squash 71

Grilled Beef in Mayonnaise with Spiralized Squash and Peanuts 73

Spiralized Cabbage and Grilled Beef in Garlic Mayonnaise 76

Spiralized Potatoes and Grilled Beef in Garlic Mayonnaise 78

Pork in Wine with Spiralized Squash and Cashews 80

Turkey Breast in Garlic Mayonnaise with Peanuts and Spiralized Beets 82

Chicken Breast in Garlic Mayonnaise with Peanuts and Spiralized Beets 85

Spicy Pork in Mustard with Peanuts, Pumpkin and Spiralized Beets 88

Inspiralized Potatoes with Lamb and Beef in Beer 91

Spiralized Zucchini with Turkey and Chicken in Beer 93

Conclusion 96

Recipe Index 97

Introduction

This book includes various meat and fish spiralizer recipes and hot spiralizer dishes (even grilled ones!) with various spiralized or grated vegetables and fruits (dried fruits and nuts as well). You will find interesting recipes that will inspire you to cook fantastic spiralized dishes. You should use your imagination because there is no limit to what you can prepare when using meat, fish and spiralized vegetables as the main ingredient. This spiralizer recipe book was created to inspire you to discover a colorful world of exotic spiralizer cooking!

Moreover, you don't need to be a professional 28 Michelin Star chef to use spiralized vegetables and meat recipes from this cookbook and to prepare grated or spiralized vegetables & meat dishes for yourself or your family. I would like to encourage you to test new spiralizer recipes and experiment by adding your own flavors!

Kitchen Utensils That You Will Need to Prepare Spiralizer Recipes

To prepare delicious spiralizer recipes you will need to have the right tools in your kitchen. The following list of kitchen tools will help you.

Spiralizer or Korean Style Carrot Grater

Spiralizer is the main tool that you will need to prepare tasty spiralized recipes. Remember that you can use Korean style grater as well.

Food Scale

The food scale is the main tool. You will use it to measure any food, especially chicken, turkey, pork, beef or lamb meat or vegetables and it will always show you the quantity of ingredients that you need for spiralizer dishes.

Food Processor or Blender

Having a food processor or blender is crucial. It will help you to process, pulse, and blend nuts, vegetables or fruits.

Electric Hand Mixer

Electric hand mixer will save your energy and of course time, especially when you are preparing spiralizer recipes where you need to combine different ingredients.

Pot, Saucepan, Frying Pan or Wok

Having a large pot, saucepan, frying pan, skillet or wok in your kitchen is crucial when preparing tasty spiralizer dishes because you will fry, bake, melt, mix and boil all the ingredients there.

Knife Sharpening Stone or Sharp Knife

When preparing spiralizer recipes you often need to chop, cut, slice or halve meat, fish, fresh veggies and fruits. In this case, having a sharp blade in your kitchen will save you a lot of time and frustrations because you will finish cutting up your ingredients much faster than you would if using a dull knife.

Baking pan

Baking pan is also important because you will need it to bake the meat, potatoes, zucchini and other ingredients.

The following chapters contain tasty spiralizer recipes that will have your taste buds come to life!

Spiralized Meat & Fish Dishes

Spiralized Carrots with Shrimps, Pineapple and Raisins

Prep Time: 20 min. | Cooking Time: 40-50 min. | Servings: 4

Ingredients:

5 cups of shrimps

5 carrots, peeled and spiralized

1 pineapple, peeled and spiralized

4 garlic cloves, minced

5 tablespoons Olive oil

1 cup of raisins

salt and pepper

1 teaspoon powdered black pepper

2 tablespoons powdered garlic

1 teaspoon nutmeg, ground

1 bunch of fresh chives, chopped

How to Prepare:

1. Wash and soak the raisins in the warm water.

2. Combine the powdered black pepper, powdered garlic and some salt. Season the shrimps with the salt and pepper, and toss in the powdered garlic, and nutmeg mix. Marinate the shrimps overnight in the powdered garlic, pepper, and nutmeg.

3. Heat the water and boil the shrimps for 10 minutes. Strain the shrimps and heat the Olive oil in a frying pan or wok and fry the shrimps with the spiralized carrots for 30 minutes, until golden brown.

4. Toss the spiralized pineapple in the Olive oil. A few minutes before the shrimps are ready, mix in the spiralized pineapple and stew with the shrimps with the lid closed for around 10 minutes, until the liquid is absorbed. A few minutes before the shrimps are ready, add in the minced garlic cloves and raisins.

5. Sprinkle the chopped chives and you are free to serve the shrimps and spiralized carrots in separate dishes with the white wine. Remember that this dish should be served warm.

<u>Nutritional Information:</u>

Calories: 189; Total fat: 32 oz; Total carbohydrates: 39 oz; Protein: 19 oz

Spiralized Zucchini with Shrimps, Pineapple and Apricots

Prep Time: 20 min. | Cooking Time: 50-60 min. | Servings: 4

Ingredients:

5 cups of shrimps

3 zucchinis, peeled and spiralized

1 pineapple, peeled and spiralized

4 garlic cloves, minced

5 tablespoons Olive oil

2 cups of dried apricots

salt and pepper

1 teaspoon powdered black pepper

2 tablespoons powdered garlic

1 teaspoon nutmeg, ground

1 bunch of fresh parsley, chopped

How to Prepare:

1. Wash and soak the apricots in the warm water. Then chop the apricots. Use a knife or a food processor.

2. Combine the powdered black pepper, powdered garlic and some salt. Season the shrimps with the salt and pepper, and toss in the powdered garlic, and nutmeg mix. Marinate the shrimps overnight in the powdered garlic, pepper, and nutmeg.

3. Heat the water and boil the shrimps for 10 minutes. Strain the shrimps and heat the Olive oil in a frying pan or wok and fry the shrimps with the spiralized zucchinis for around 30 minutes, until golden brown.

4. Toss the spiralized pineapple in the Olive oil. A few minutes before the shrimps are ready, mix in the spiralized pineapple and stew with the shrimps with the lid closed for around 10-20 minutes, until the liquid is absorbed. A few minutes before the shrimps are ready, mix in the minced garlic cloves and chopped apricots.

5. Sprinkle the chopped parsley and you are free to serve the shrimps and spiralized zucchinis in separate dishes with the white wine. Remember that this dish should be served warm.

Nutritional Information:

Calories: 191; Total fat: 33 oz; Total carbohydrates: 40 oz; Protein: 22 oz

Spiralized Potatoes with Shrimps, Pineapple and Celery

Prep Time: 20 min. | Cooking Time: 50-60 min. | Servings: 6

Ingredients:

6 cups of shrimps

8 potatoes, peeled and spiralized

5 oz noodles,

1 pineapple, peeled and spiralized

4 garlic cloves, minced

5 tablespoons Olive oil

2 cups of celery, chopped

salt and pepper

1 teaspoon powdered black pepper

2 tablespoons powdered garlic

1 teaspoon nutmeg, ground

1 bunch of fresh parsley, chopped

How to Prepare:

1. Boil the water and cook the noodles for 20 minutes or follow the cooking time suggested on the packet. Add 1 tablespoon Olive oil.

2. Combine the powdered black pepper, powdered garlic and some salt. Season the shrimps with the salt and pepper, and toss in the powdered garlic, and nutmeg mix. Marinate the shrimps overnight in the powdered garlic, pepper, and nutmeg.

3. Heat the water and boil the shrimps for 10 minutes. Strain the shrimps and heat the Olive oil in a frying pan or wok and fry the shrimps with the spiralized potatoes for around 30 minutes, until golden brown.

4. Toss the spiralized pineapple in the Olive oil. A few minutes before the shrimps are ready, mix in the spiralized pineapple and stew with the shrimps with the lid closed for around 10-20 minutes, until the liquid is absorbed. A few minutes

before the shrimps are ready, mix in the minced garlic cloves and chopped celery.

5. Add in the noodles. Sprinkle the chopped parsley and you are free to serve the shrimps and spiralized potatoes in separate dishes with the white wine. Remember that this dish should be served warm.

Nutritional Information:

Calories: 195; Total fat: 35 oz; Total carbohydrates: 45 oz; Protein: 25 oz

Spiralized Squash with Shrimps, Carrots and Plums

Prep Time: 25 min. | Cooking Time: 60-70 min. | Servings: 5

Ingredients:

5 cups of shrimps

5 cups of squash, peeled and spiralized

3 carrots, peeled and spiralized

3 cups of dried plums

5 garlic cloves, minced

6 tablespoons sunflower oil

3 onions, peeled and chopped

salt and pepper

1 teaspoon powdered black pepper

2 tablespoons powdered garlic

1 teaspoon nutmeg, ground

1 bunch of fresh parsley, chopped

How to Prepare:

1. Combine the powdered black pepper, powdered garlic, garlic cloves and some salt. Season the shrimps with the salt and pepper, and toss in the powdered garlic, garlic and nutmeg

mix. Marinate the shrimps overnight in the powdered garlic, garlic, pepper, and nutmeg.

2. Heat the water and boil the shrimps for 20 minutes. Strain the shrimps and heat the sunflower oil in a frying pan or wok and fry the shrimps with the spiralized squash for around 30 minutes.

3. Toss the spiralized carrots in the sunflower oil. A few minutes before the shrimps are ready, mix in the spiralized carrots and stew with the shrimps with the lid closed for around 10-20 minutes, until the liquid is absorbed. A few minutes before the shrimps are ready, mix in the chopped onions and dried plums.

4. Sprinkle the chopped parsley and you are free to serve the shrimps and spiralized squash in separate dishes with the beer. Remember that this dish should be served warm.

Nutritional Information:

Calories: 191; Total fat: 33 oz; Total carbohydrates: 43 oz; Protein: 24 oz

Spiralized Cabbage with Shrimps, Onions and Plums

Prep Time: 25 min. | Cooking Time: 60-70 min. | Servings: 7

Ingredients:

7 cups of shrimps

1 big cabbage, spiralized

5 big onions, peeled and spiralized

3 cups of dried plums

5 garlic cloves, minced

6 tablespoons sunflower oil

salt and pepper

1 teaspoon powdered black pepper

2 tablespoons powdered garlic

1 teaspoon basil, ground

1 bunch of fresh parsley, chopped

How to Prepare:

1. Combine the powdered black pepper, powdered garlic, garlic cloves and some salt. Season the shrimps with the salt and pepper, and toss in the powdered garlic, garlic and basil mix.

Marinate the shrimps overnight in the powdered garlic, garlic, pepper, and basil.

2. Heat the water and boil the shrimps for 20 minutes. Strain the shrimps and heat the sunflower oil in a frying pan or wok and fry the shrimps with the spiralized cabbage for around 30 minutes.

3. Toss the spiralized onions in the sunflower oil. A few minutes before the shrimps are ready, mix in the spiralized onions and stew with the shrimps with the lid closed for around 10-20 minutes, until the liquid is absorbed. A few minutes before the shrimps are ready, mix in the dried plums.

4. Sprinkle the chopped parsley and you are free to serve the shrimps and spiralized cabbage in separate plates. Remember that this dish should be served warm.

Nutritional Information:

Calories: 192; Total fat: 34 oz; Total carbohydrates: 44 oz; Protein: 25 oz

Inspiralized Carrots with Beef, Milk and Walnuts

Prep Time: 20 min. | Cooking Time: 40-50 min. | Servings: 4

Ingredients:

15 oz beef, cubed

1 cup of milk

1 cup of walnuts

8 big carrots, peeled and spiralized

5 tablespoons Olive oil

5 tablespoons freshly squeezed lemon juice

1 teaspoon powdered red pepper

2 tablespoons powdered garlic

1 teaspoon nutmeg, ground

salt and pepper

How to Prepare:

1. Preheat the oven to 220°-250° Fahrenheit and roast the walnuts in the oven for around 10 minutes until lightly browned and crispy. Grind them using a food processor.

2. In a bowl, combine powdered red pepper, powdered garlic, nutmeg, and some salt. Season the beef cubes with the salt and pepper, and toss in the powdered garlic, powdered red pepper, and nutmeg mix. Set the meat aside to marinate it overnight in milk.

3. Preheat the oven to 320°-360° Fahrenheit, and bake the cubed beef meat for around 40-50 minutes until golden brown and crispy. Toss the spiralized carrots in the Olive oil and salt. A few minutes before the beef is ready add in the spiralized carrots and bake it with the beef chunks.

4. Sprinkle the walnuts over the spiralized carrots and baked beef chunks.

5. Sprinkle the salt and pepper and pour the freshly squeezed lemon juice over the beef and you are free to serve the spiralized carrots with beef in separate plates with a white wine. Remember that this dish should be served warm.

Nutritional Information:

Calories: 289; Total fat: 44 oz; Total carbohydrates: 65 oz; Protein: 35 oz

Inspiralized Zucchini with Beef, Milk and Peanuts

Prep Time: 20 min. | Cooking Time: 50-60 min. | Servings: 4

Ingredients:

20 oz beef, cubed

1.5 cups of milk

1 cup of peanuts

2 big zucchinis, peeled and spiralized

5 tablespoons Olive oil

5 tablespoons freshly squeezed lemon juice

1 teaspoon powdered red pepper

2 tablespoons powdered garlic

1 teaspoon nutmeg, ground

salt and pepper

How to Prepare:

1. Preheat the oven to 220°-250° Fahrenheit and roast the peanuts in the oven for around 10 minutes until lightly browned and crispy.

2. In a bowl, combine powdered red pepper, powdered garlic, nutmeg, and some salt. Season the beef cubes with the salt and pepper, and toss in the powdered garlic, powdered red pepper, and nutmeg mix. Set the meat aside to marinate it overnight in milk.

3. Preheat the oven to 320°-340° Fahrenheit, and bake the cubed beef meat for around 40-60 minutes until golden brown and crispy. Toss the spiralized zucchini in the Olive oil and salt. A few minutes before the beef is ready add in the spiralized zucchini and bake it with the beef chunks.

4. Spoon the peanuts over the spiralized zucchini and baked beef chunks.

5. Sprinkle the salt and pepper and pour the freshly squeezed lemon juice over the beef and you are free to serve the

spiralized zucchini with beef in separate plates with a white wine. Remember that this dish should be served warm.

Nutritional Information:

Calories: 294; Total fat: 45 oz; Total carbohydrates: 67 oz; Protein: 37 oz

Spiralized Potatoes with Beef, Beer and Walnuts

Prep Time: 20 min. | Cooking Time: 40-50 min. | Servings: 5

Ingredients:

25 oz beef, cubed

2 cups of beer

1 cup of walnuts

10 potatoes, peeled and spiralized

5 tablespoons Olive oil

5 tablespoons freshly squeezed lemon juice

1 teaspoon powdered red pepper

2 tablespoons powdered garlic

1 teaspoon nutmeg, ground

salt and pepper

How to Prepare:

1. Preheat the oven to 220°-250° Fahrenheit and roast the walnuts in the oven for around 10 minutes until lightly browned and crispy. Grind them using a food processor.

2. In a bowl, combine powdered red pepper, powdered garlic, nutmeg, and some salt. Season the beef cubes with the salt and pepper, and toss in the powdered garlic, powdered red pepper, and nutmeg mix. Set the meat aside to marinate it overnight in beer.

3. Preheat the oven to 320°-360° Fahrenheit, and bake the cubed beef meat with the spiralized potatoes for around 40-50 minutes until golden brown and crispy.

4. Spoon the walnuts over the spiralized potatoes and baked beef chunks.

5. Sprinkle the salt and pepper and pour the freshly squeezed lemon juice over the beef and you are free to serve the spiralized potatoes with beef in separate plates. Remember that this dish should be served warm.

Nutritional Information:

Calories: 294; Total fat: 46 oz; Total carbohydrates: 67 oz; Protein: 37 oz

Spiralized Squash with Pork, Beer and Peanuts

Prep Time: 20 min. | Cooking Time: 40-50 min. | Servings: 4

Ingredients:

20 oz pork, cubed

2 cups of beer

2 cups of peanuts

1 big squash, peeled and spiralized

5 tablespoons Olive oil

5 tablespoons freshly squeezed lemon juice

1 teaspoon powdered red pepper

2 tablespoons powdered garlic

1 teaspoon nutmeg, ground

salt and pepper

How to Prepare:

1. Preheat the oven to 220°-250° Fahrenheit and roast the peanuts in the oven for around 10 minutes until lightly browned and crispy. Grind them using a food processor.

2. In a bowl, combine powdered red pepper, powdered garlic, nutmeg, and some salt. Season the pork cubes with the salt and pepper, and toss in the powdered garlic, powdered red pepper, and nutmeg mix. Set the meat aside to marinate it overnight in beer.

3. Preheat the oven to 320°-340° Fahrenheit, and bake the cubed pork meat for around 40-50 minutes until golden brown and crispy. Toss the spiralized squash in the Olive oil and salt. A 10 minutes before the pork is ready add in the spiralized squash and bake it with the pork chunks.

4. Spoon the peanuts over the spiralized squash and baked pork chunks.

5. Sprinkle the salt and pepper and pour the freshly squeezed lemon juice over the pork and you are free to serve the spiralized squash with pork in separate plates. Remember that this dish should be served warm with the red or white wine.

Nutritional Information:

Calories: 295; Total fat: 45 oz; Total carbohydrates: 65 oz; Protein: 36 oz

Spiralized Cabbage with Pork, Beer and Peanuts

Prep Time: 20 min. | Cooking Time: 40-50 min. | Servings: 4

Ingredients:

20 oz pork, cubed

2 cups of beer

2 cups of peanuts

1 big cabbage, peeled and spiralized

5 tablespoons Olive oil

5 tablespoons freshly squeezed lemon juice

1 teaspoon powdered red pepper

2 tablespoons powdered garlic

1 teaspoon nutmeg, ground

salt and pepper

How to Prepare:

1. Preheat the oven to 220°-250° Fahrenheit and roast the peanuts in the oven for around 10 minutes until lightly browned and crispy. Grind them using a food processor.

2. In a bowl, combine powdered red pepper, powdered garlic, nutmeg, and some salt. Season the pork cubes with the salt and pepper, and toss in the powdered garlic, powdered red pepper, and nutmeg mix. Set the meat aside to marinate it overnight in beer.

3. Preheat the oven to 320°-340° Fahrenheit, and bake the cubed pork meat for around 40-50 minutes until golden brown and crispy. Toss the spiralized cabbage in the Olive oil and salt. A 10 minutes before the pork is ready add in the spiralized cabbage and bake it with the pork chunks.

4. Spoon the peanuts over the spiralized cabbage and baked pork chunks.

5. Sprinkle the salt and pepper and pour the freshly squeezed lemon juice over the pork and you are free to serve the

spiralized cabbage with pork in separate plates. Remember that this dish should be served warm with the red wine.

<u>Nutritional Information:</u>

Calories: 297; Total fat: 46 oz; Total carbohydrates: 67 oz; Protein: 37 oz

Spiralized Cabbage with Turkey and Cashews

Prep Time: 25 min. | Cooking Time: 50-60 min. | Servings: 4

Ingredients:

3 cups of turkey breast, cubed

1 cup of cashews

1 cabbage, spiralized

5 tomatoes, cubed

6 tablespoons Olive oil

4 tablespoons freshly squeezed lemon juice

1 teaspoon powdered red pepper

2 tablespoons powdered garlic

1 teaspoon nutmeg, ground

salt and pepper

How to Prepare:

1. Preheat the oven to 220°-250° Fahrenheit and roast the cashews in the oven for around 10 minutes until lightly browned and crispy.

2. In a bowl, combine powdered red pepper, powdered garlic, nutmeg, and some salt. Season the turkey cubes with the salt and pepper, and toss in the powdered garlic, powdered red pepper, and nutmeg mix. Set aside and marinate the turkey meat overnight in the fridge.

3. Heat the Olive oil in a frying pan or wok and fry the turkey cubes for around 20 minutes until soft and golden brown. Preheat the oven to 300°-320° Fahrenheit, and bake the cubed turkey for around 40-50 minutes until golden brown and crispy. Toss the spiralized cabbage in the Olive oil and salt. A few minutes before the turkey is ready add in the spiralized cabbage and bake it with the turkey chunks.

4. Combine the cashews with the cubed tomatoes and spoon over the spiralized cabbage and baked turkey chunks.

5. Sprinkle the salt and pepper and pour the freshly squeezed lemon juice over the turkey and you are free to serve the spiralized cabbage with turkey in separate plates with the white wine. Remember that this dish should be served warm.

Nutritional Information:

Calories: 263; Total fat: 30 oz; Total carbohydrates: 57 oz; Protein: 25 oz

Spiralized Potatoes with Turkey and Zucchini

Prep Time: 25 min. | Cooking Time: 50-60 min. | Servings: 5

Ingredients:

4 cups of turkey breast, cubed

10 potatoes, peeled and cubed

1 cabbage, spiralized

5 tomatoes, cubed

6 tablespoons Olive oil

4 tablespoons freshly squeezed lemon juice

1 teaspoon powdered red pepper

2 tablespoons powdered garlic

1 teaspoon nutmeg, ground

salt and pepper

How to Prepare:

1. In a bowl, combine powdered red pepper, powdered garlic, nutmeg, and some salt. Season the turkey cubes with the salt and pepper, and toss in the powdered garlic, powdered red pepper, and nutmeg mix. Set aside and marinate the turkey meat overnight in the fridge.

2. Heat the Olive oil in a frying pan or wok and fry the turkey cubes for around 20 minutes until soft and golden brown. Preheat the oven to 300°-320° Fahrenheit, and bake the cubed turkey with the potatoes for around 40-50 minutes until golden brown and crispy. Toss the spiralized cabbage in the Olive oil and salt. 10 minutes before the turkey is ready add in the spiralized cabbage and bake it with the turkey chunks and potatoes.

3. Mix in the cubed tomatoes and sprinkle the salt and pepper. Pour the freshly squeezed lemon juice over the turkey breast and you are free to serve the spiralized potatoes with turkey in separate plates with the white wine. Remember that this dish should be served warm.

Nutritional Information:

Calories: 264; Total fat: 31 oz; Total carbohydrates: 58 oz; Protein: 27 oz

Spiralized Potatoes with Chicken and Carrots

Prep Time: 25 min. | Cooking Time: 50-60 min. | Servings: 5

Ingredients:

5 cups of chicken, cubed

10 potatoes, peeled and cubed

5 carrots, peeled and spiralized

5 tomatoes, cubed

6 tablespoons Olive oil

4 tablespoons freshly squeezed lemon juice

1 teaspoon powdered red pepper

2 tablespoons powdered garlic

1 teaspoon nutmeg, ground

salt and pepper

How to Prepare:

1. In a bowl, combine powdered red pepper, powdered garlic, nutmeg, and some salt. Season the chicken cubes with the salt and pepper, and toss in the powdered garlic, powdered red pepper, and nutmeg mix. Set aside and marinate the chicken meat overnight in the fridge.

2. Heat the Olive oil in a frying pan or wok and fry the chicken cubes for around 20 minutes until soft and golden brown. Preheat the oven to 300°-320° Fahrenheit, and bake the cubed chicken with the potatoes for around 40-50 minutes until golden brown and crispy. Toss the spiralized carrots in the Olive oil and salt. 10 minutes before the chicken is ready add in the spiralized carrots and bake it with the chicken chunks and potatoes.

3. Mix in the cubed tomatoes and sprinkle the salt and pepper. Pour the freshly squeezed lemon juice over the chicken and you are free to serve the spiralized potatoes with chicken in separate plates with the white wine. Remember that this dish should be served warm.

Nutritional Information:

Calories: 265; Total fat: 33 oz; Total carbohydrates: 59 oz; Protein: 29 oz

Inspiralized Onions with Lamb and Mayonnaise

Prep Time: 25 min. | Cooking Time: 60-70 min. | Servings: 4

Ingredients:

4 lamb chunks

10 onions, peeled and spiralized

3 carrots, peeled and spiralized

2 cups of mayonnaise

6 tablespoons Olive oil

4 tablespoons freshly squeezed lemon juice

1 teaspoon powdered red pepper

2 tablespoons powdered garlic

1 teaspoon nutmeg, ground

salt and pepper

How to Prepare:

1. In a bowl, combine powdered red pepper, powdered garlic, nutmeg, and some salt. Season the lamb with the salt and pepper, and toss in the powdered garlic, powdered red pepper, nutmeg and mayonnaise mix. Set aside and marinate the lamb meat overnight in the fridge.

2. Heat the Olive oil in a frying pan or wok and fry the lamb for around 20 minutes. Preheat the oven to 300°-320° Fahrenheit, and bake the lamb for around 60-70 minutes until golden brown and soft. Toss the spiralized carrots and onions in the Olive oil and salt. 20 minutes before the lamb is ready add in the spiralized onions and carrots and bake them with the lamb.

3. Pour the freshly squeezed lemon juice over the lamb and you are free to serve the spiralized onions with the lamb in separate plates with the white wine. Remember that this dish should be served warm.

Nutritional Information:

Calories: 375; Total fat: 69 oz; Total carbohydrates: 79 oz; Protein: 56 oz

Inspiralized Onions with Lamb and Wine

Prep Time: 25 min. | Cooking Time: 60-70 min. | Servings: 4

Ingredients:

15 oz lamb, cubed

10 onions, peeled and spiralized

3 carrots, peeled and spiralized

1 bottle of white wine

6 tablespoons Olive oil

4 tablespoons freshly squeezed lemon juice

1 teaspoon powdered red pepper

2 tablespoons powdered garlic

1 teaspoon nutmeg, ground

salt and pepper

How to Prepare:

1. In a bowl, combine powdered red pepper, powdered garlic, nutmeg, and some salt. Season the lamb with the salt and pepper, and toss in the powdered garlic, powdered red pepper and nutmeg mix. Set aside and marinate the lamb meat overnight in the white wine.

2. Heat the Olive oil in a frying pan or wok and fry the lamb for around 20 minutes. Preheat the oven to 300°-320° Fahrenheit, and bake the lamb for around 60-70 minutes until golden brown and soft. Toss the spiralized carrots and onions in the Olive oil and salt. 20 minutes before the lamb is ready mix in the spiralized onions and carrots and bake them with the lamb.
3. Pour the freshly squeezed lemon juice over the lamb and you are free to serve the spiralized onions with the lamb in separate plates with the white wine. Remember that this dish should be served warm.

Nutritional Information:

Calories: 375; Total fat: 67 oz; Total carbohydrates: 72 oz; Protein: 54 oz

Salmon in Mayonnaise and Spiralized Zucchini

Prep Time: 25 min. | Cooking Time: 20-30 min. | Servings: 2

Ingredients:

10 oz salmon, sliced

1 cup of mayonnaise

1 zucchini, peeled and spiralized

4 tomatoes, cubed

4 garlic cloves, minced

5 tablespoons Olive oil

4 tablespoons soy sauce

5 tablespoons freshly squeezed lemon juice

1 teaspoon powdered chili pepper

3 tablespoons powdered garlic

salt and pepper

How to Prepare:

1. In a bowl, combine powdered chili pepper, powdered garlic, minced garlic cloves, and some salt. Season the salmon with the salt and pepper, and toss in the powdered garlic and powdered chili pepper mix. Spoon the mayonnaise over the salmon and marinate the fish for at least 10 hours in the fridge.

2. Heat the Olive oil in a frying pan or wok and fry the salmon for around 10 minutes until soft. Preheat the oven to 300°-330° Fahrenheit, and bake the salmon for around 20-30 minutes until golden brown. Toss the spiralized zucchini in the Olive oil and salt. Few minutes before the salmon is ready add in the spiralized zucchini and bake it with the salmon.

3. Combine the soy sauce with the cubed tomatoes and spoon over the spiralized zucchini and salmon.

4. Sprinkle the salt and pepper and pour the freshly squeezed lemon juice over the spiralized zucchini and salmon and you are free to serve the salmon and spiralized zucchini in

separate bowls. Remember that this dish should be served warm.

Nutritional Information:

Calories: 262; Total fat: 38 oz; Total carbohydrates: 55 oz; Protein: 29 oz

Tuna in Garlic Mayonnaise with Peanuts and Spiralized Zucchini

---

Prep Time: 25 min. | Cooking Time: 40-50 min. | Servings: 2

Ingredients:

10 oz tuna, cubed

2 cups of peanuts

1 cup of garlic mayonnaise

1 zucchini, peeled and spiralized

4 tomatoes, cubed

5 garlic cloves, minced

5 tablespoons Olive oil

4 tablespoons soy sauce

5 tablespoons freshly squeezed lemon juice

1 teaspoon powdered chili pepper

3 tablespoons powdered garlic

salt and pepper

How to Prepare:

1. Preheat the oven to 230°-260° Fahrenheit and roast the peanuts in the oven for around 10 minutes until lightly browned and crispy.

2. In a bowl, combine powdered chili pepper, powdered garlic, and some salt. Season the tuna cubes with the salt and pepper, and toss in the powdered garlic and powdered chili pepper mix. Spoon the garlic mayonnaise over the tuna and marinate the fish for at least 10 hours in the fridge.

3. Heat the Olive oil in a frying pan or wok and fry the tuna cubes for around 10 minutes until soft. Preheat the oven to 300°-330° Fahrenheit, and bake the cubed tuna for around 30-40 minutes until golden brown. Toss the spiralized zucchini in the Olive oil and salt. Few minutes before the tuna is ready add in the spiralized zucchini and bake it with the tuna cubes.

4. Combine the soy sauce with the cubed tomatoes, peanuts and minced garlic cloves and spoon over the spiralized zucchini and tuna cubes.

5. Sprinkle the salt and pepper and pour the freshly squeezed lemon juice over the spiralized zucchini and tuna cubes and you are free to serve the spiralized zucchini and tuna in

separate bowls. Remember that this dish should be served warm.

Nutritional Information:

Calories: 268; Total fat: 42 oz; Total carbohydrates: 59 oz; Protein: 31 oz

Garlic Tuna and Spiralized Squash

Prep Time: 25 min. | Cooking Time: 40-50 min. | Servings: 3

Ingredients:

15 oz tuna, cubed

1 cup of garlic mayonnaise

5 garlic cloves, minced

4 tablespoons powdered garlic

1 squash, peeled and spiralized

4 tomatoes, cubed

5 tablespoons Olive oil

4 tablespoons soy sauce

5 tablespoons freshly squeezed lemon juice

1 teaspoon powdered chili pepper

salt and pepper

How to Prepare:

1. In a bowl, combine powdered chili pepper, powdered garlic, minced garlic cloves, and some salt. Season the tuna cubes with the salt and pepper, and toss in the powdered garlic, garlic and powdered chili pepper mix. Spoon the garlic mayonnaise over the tuna and marinate the fish overnight in the mayonnaise and spices.

2. Heat the Olive oil in a frying pan or wok and stew the tuna cubes with the lid closed for around 10 minutes until soft. Preheat the oven to 300°-330° Fahrenheit, and bake the cubed tuna for around 30-40 minutes until golden brown. Toss the spiralized squash in the Olive oil and salt. Few minutes before the tuna is ready add in the spiralized squash and bake it with the tuna cubes.

3. Combine the soy sauce with the cubed tomatoes and spoon over the spiralized squash and tuna cubes.

4. Sprinkle the salt and pepper and pour the freshly squeezed lemon juice over the spiralized squash and tuna cubes and you are free to serve the spiralized squash with tuna in

separate bowls. Remember that this dish should be served warm.

Nutritional Information:

Calories: 265; Total fat: 39 oz; Total carbohydrates: 54 oz; Protein: 27 oz

Tuna in Garlic Mayonnaise with Walnuts and Spiralized Zucchini

Prep Time: 25 min. | Cooking Time: 40-50 min. | Servings: 2

Ingredients:

10 oz tuna, cubed

2 cups of walnuts

1 cup of garlic mayonnaise

1 zucchini, peeled and spiralized

4 tomatoes, cubed

5 garlic cloves, minced

5 tablespoons Olive oil

4 tablespoons soy sauce

5 tablespoons freshly squeezed lemon juice

1 teaspoon powdered chili pepper

3 tablespoons powdered garlic

salt and pepper

How to Prepare:

1. Preheat the oven to 230°-260° Fahrenheit and roast the walnuts in the oven for around 10 minutes until lightly

browned and crispy. Grind the walnuts using a food processor.

2. In a bowl, combine powdered chili pepper, powdered garlic, and some salt. Season the tuna cubes with the salt and pepper, and toss in the powdered garlic and powdered chili pepper mix. Spoon the garlic mayonnaise over the tuna and marinate the fish overnight in mayonnaise and spices.

3. Heat the Olive oil in a frying pan or wok and fry the tuna cubes for around 10 minutes until soft. Preheat the oven to 300°-330° Fahrenheit, and bake the cubed tuna for around 30-40 minutes until golden brown. Toss the spiralized zucchini in the Olive oil and salt. Few minutes before the tuna is ready add in the spiralized zucchini and bake it with the tuna cubes.

4. Combine the soy sauce with the cubed tomatoes, walnuts and minced garlic cloves and spoon over the spiralized zucchini and tuna cubes.

5. Sprinkle the salt and pepper and pour the freshly squeezed lemon juice over the spiralized zucchini and tuna cubes and you are free to serve the spiralized zucchini and tuna in separate bowls. Remember that this dish should be served warm.

Nutritional Information:

Calories: 270; Total fat: 45 oz; Total carbohydrates: 60 oz; Protein: 32 oz

Hake in Garlic Mayonnaise with Peanuts and Spiralized Carrots

---

Prep Time: 30 min. | Cooking Time: 50-60 min. | Servings: 4

Ingredients:

20 oz hake, cubed

2 cups of peanuts

2 cups of garlic mayonnaise

5 carrots, peeled and spiralized

2 onions, spiralized

5 tablespoons Olive oil

4 tablespoons soy sauce

5 tablespoons freshly squeezed lemon juice

1 teaspoon powdered chili pepper

3 tablespoons powdered garlic

salt and pepper

How to Prepare:

1. Preheat the oven to 230°-260° Fahrenheit and roast the peanuts in the oven for around 10 minutes until lightly browned and crispy.

2. In a bowl, combine powdered chili pepper, powdered garlic, and some salt. Season the hake cubes with the salt and pepper, and toss in the powdered garlic and powdered chili pepper mix. Spoon the garlic mayonnaise over the hake and marinate the fish for at least 10 hours.

3. Heat the Olive oil in a frying pan or wok and fry the hake cubes for around 20 minutes until soft. Preheat the oven to 290°-320° Fahrenheit, and bake the cubed hake for around 30-40 minutes. Toss the spiralized carrots and onions in the Olive oil and salt. 20 minutes before the hake is ready add in the spiralized carrots and onions and bake them with the hake cubes.

4. Combine the soy sauce with the peanuts and spoon over the spiralized carrots and hake cubes.

5. Sprinkle the salt and pepper and pour the freshly squeezed lemon juice over the spiralized carrots and hake cubes and you are free to serve the spiralized carrots and hake in separate bowls. Remember that this dish should be served warm.

Nutritional Information:

Calories: 269; Total fat: 43 oz; Total carbohydrates: 60 oz; Protein: 32 oz

Grilled Lamb in Garlic Mayonnaise with Spiralized Zucchini and Celery

Prep Time: 20 min. | Cooking Time: 50-60 min. | Servings: 3

Ingredients:

15 oz lamb, cubed

2 cups of garlic mayonnaise

1 zucchini, peeled and spiralized

2 cups of celery, cubed

5 tablespoons Olive oil

3 tablespoons soy sauce

5 tablespoons freshly squeezed lemon juice

1 teaspoon powdered chili pepper

2 tablespoons powdered garlic

nutmeg

salt and pepper

How to Prepare:

1. In a bowl, combine powdered chili pepper, powdered garlic, nutmeg, garlic mayonnaise and some salt. Season the lamb with the salt and pepper, and toss in the powdered garlic, garlic mayonnaise and powdered chili pepper mix. Place the lamb into a pot or bowl and marinate the meat overnight in mayonnaise and spices.

2. Toss the spiralized zucchini and celery in the Olive oil and salt. Heat the Olive oil in a frying pan or wok and fry the spiralized zucchini and celery for around 10 minutes until soft and then stew with the lid closed for around 5 minutes until the liquid is absorbed.

3. Grill the lamb meat until golden brown and crispy. Spoon the soy sauce over the grilled lamb. Then spoon the spiralized zucchini and celery on top.

4. Sprinkle the salt and pepper and pour the freshly squeezed lemon juice over the spiralized zucchini and grilled lamb and

you are free to serve the grilled meat. Remember that this dish should be served warm.

Nutritional Information:

Calories: 358; Total fat: 77 oz; Total carbohydrates: 95 oz; Protein: 59 oz

Grilled Shrimps with Spiralized Zucchini (Cover Recipe)

Prep Time: 20 min. | Cooking Time: 30-45 min. | Servings: 4

Ingredients:

5 cups of big shrimps

1 zucchini, peeled and spiralized

5 tomatoes, cubed

5 tablespoons Olive oil, 3 tablespoons soy sauce

5 tablespoons freshly squeezed lemon juice

1 teaspoon powdered chili pepper

2 tablespoons powdered garlic

½ teaspoon oregano, salt and pepper

How to Prepare:

1. In a bowl, combine powdered chili pepper, powdered garlic, oregano and some salt. Season the shrimps with the salt and pepper, and toss in the powdered garlic, oregano and powdered chili pepper mix. Set the shrimps aside and marinate them for at least 5 hours unrefrigerated at room temperature or place in the fridge overnight.
2. Toss the spiralized zucchini in the Olive oil and salt. Heat the Olive oil in a frying pan or wok and fry the spiralized zucchini for around 10 minutes until soft, then stew with the lid closed for around 10 minutes until the liquid is absorbed.
3. Grill the shrimps until golden brown and crispy. Combine the soy sauce with the cubed tomatoes and spoon over the grilled shrimps. Then spoon the spiralized zucchini on top and mix well.
4. Sprinkle the salt and pepper and pour the freshly squeezed lemon juice over the spiralized zucchini and grilled shrimps and you are free to serve the spiralized zucchini and shrimps in separate dishes. Remember that this dish should be served warm.

Nutritional Information:

Calories: 256; Total fat: 44 oz; Total carbohydrates: 63 oz; Protein: 32 oz

Grilled Shrimps with Oranges and Spiralized Pineapple

Prep Time: 20 min. | Cooking Time: 30-45 min. | Servings: 4

Ingredients:

5 cups of big shrimps

1 pineapple, peeled and spiralized

5 oranges, peeled and cubed

5 tablespoons Olive oil

2 tablespoons soy sauce

5 tablespoons freshly squeezed orange juice

1 teaspoon powdered chili pepper

2 tablespoons powdered garlic

½ teaspoon oregano

salt and pepper

How to Prepare:

1. In a bowl, combine powdered chili pepper, powdered garlic, oregano and some salt. Season the shrimps with the salt and pepper, and toss in the powdered garlic, oregano and powdered chili pepper mix. Set the shrimps aside and

marinate them for at least 5 hours unrefrigerated at room temperature or place in the fridge overnight.

2. Heat the Olive oil in a frying pan or wok and fry the spiralized pineapple for around 10 minutes until soft, then stew with the lid closed for around 10 minutes until the liquid is absorbed.

3. Grill the shrimps until golden brown and crispy. Spoon the soy sauce over the grilled shrimps. Then spoon the oranges and spiralized pineapple on top and mix well.

4. Sprinkle the salt and pepper and pour the freshly squeezed orange juice over the spiralized pineapple and grilled shrimps and you are free to serve the shrimps in separate dishes. Remember that this dish should be served warm.

Nutritional Information:

Calories: 251; Total fat: 42 oz; Total carbohydrates: 57 oz; Protein: 29 oz

Grilled Chicken with Oranges and Spiralized Pineapple

Prep Time: 20 min. | Cooking Time: 30-45 min. | Servings: 4

Ingredients:

15 oz chicken, cubed

1 pineapple, peeled and spiralized

5 oranges, peeled and cubed

5 tablespoons Olive oil

2 tablespoons soy sauce

5 tablespoons freshly squeezed orange juice

1 teaspoon powdered chili pepper

2 tablespoons powdered garlic

½ teaspoon oregano

salt and pepper

How to Prepare:

1. In a bowl, combine powdered chili pepper, powdered garlic, oregano and some salt. Season the chicken with the salt and pepper, and toss in the powdered garlic, oregano and powdered chili pepper mix. Set the chicken aside and marinate it overnight in spices.

2. Heat the Olive oil in a frying pan or wok and fry the spiralized pineapple for around 5 minutes until soft, then stew with the lid closed for around 5 minutes until the liquid is absorbed.

3. Grill the chicken until golden brown and crispy. Spoon the soy sauce over the grilled chicken. Then spoon the oranges and spiralized pineapple on top and mix well.

4. Sprinkle the salt and pepper and pour the freshly squeezed orange juice over the spiralized pineapple and grilled chicken and you are free to serve the chicken. Remember that this dish should be served warm.

Nutritional Information:

Calories: 265; Total fat: 43 oz; Total carbohydrates: 59 oz; Protein: 35 oz

Grilled Pork in Mayonnaise with Spiralized Squash

Prep Time: 20 min. | Cooking Time: 30-45 min. | Servings: 4

Ingredients:

15 oz pork, cubed

1 squash, peeled and spiralized

5 cups of mayonnaise

5 tablespoons Olive oil

2 tablespoons soy sauce

5 tablespoons freshly squeezed orange juice

1 teaspoon powdered chili pepper

2 tablespoons powdered garlic

½ teaspoon oregano

salt and pepper

How to Prepare:

1. In a bowl, combine powdered chili pepper, powdered garlic, oregano, mayonnaise and some salt. Season the pork with the salt and pepper, and toss in the powdered garlic, oregano, mayonnaise and powdered chili pepper mix. Set the

pork aside and marinate it overnight in spices and mayonnaise.

2. Heat the Olive oil in a frying pan or wok and fry the spiralized squash for around 5 minutes until soft, then stew with the lid closed for around 5 minutes until the liquid is absorbed.

3. Grill the pork until golden brown and crispy. Spoon the soy sauce over the grilled pork. Then spoon the spiralized squash on top and mix well.

4. Sprinkle the salt and pepper and pour the freshly squeezed orange juice over the spiralized squash and grilled pork and you are free to serve the grilled meat. Remember that this dish should be served warm.

Nutritional Information:

Calories: 295; Total fat: 55 oz; Total carbohydrates: 74 oz; Protein: 45 oz

Grilled Beef in Mayonnaise with Spiralized Squash and Peanuts

Prep Time: 20 min. | Cooking Time: 40-50 min. | Servings: 5

Ingredients:

25 oz beef, cubed

1 squash, peeled and spiralized

5 cups of mayonnaise

2 cups of peanuts

5 tablespoons Olive oil

2 tablespoons soy sauce

5 tablespoons freshly squeezed orange juice

1 teaspoon powdered chili pepper

2 tablespoons powdered garlic

½ teaspoon oregano

salt and pepper

How to Prepare:

1. Preheat the oven to 250°-280° Fahrenheit and roast the peanuts in the oven for around 10 minutes until lightly browned and crispy.

2. In a bowl, combine powdered chili pepper, powdered garlic, oregano, mayonnaise and some salt. Season the beef with the salt and pepper, and toss in the powdered garlic, oregano, mayonnaise and powdered chili pepper mix. Marinate the beef overnight in spices and mayonnaise.

3. Heat the Olive oil in a frying pan or wok and fry the spiralized squash for around 5 minutes until soft, then stew with the lid closed for around 5 minutes until the liquid is absorbed.

4. Grill the beef until golden brown and crispy. Spoon the soy sauce over the grilled beef. Then spoon the spiralized squash and peanuts on top and mix well.

5. Sprinkle the salt and pepper and pour the freshly squeezed orange juice over the spiralized squash and grilled beef and you are free to serve the grilled meat. Remember that this dish should be served warm.

Nutritional Information:

Calories: 325; Total fat: 65 oz; Total carbohydrates: 79 oz; Protein: 43 oz

Spiralized Cabbage and Grilled Beef in Garlic Mayonnaise

Prep Time: 20 min. | Cooking Time: 40-50 min. | Servings: 5

Ingredients:

25 oz beef, cubed

1 cabbage, peeled and spiralized

5 cups of garlic mayonnaise

5 tablespoons Olive oil

2 tablespoons soy sauce

5 tablespoons freshly squeezed lemon juice

1 teaspoon black pepper

3 tablespoons powdered garlic

½ teaspoon nutmeg

salt and pepper

How to Prepare:

1. In a bowl, combine powdered garlic, pepper, nutmeg, garlic mayonnaise and some salt. Season the beef with the salt and pepper, and toss in the powdered garlic, nutmeg and garlic mayonnaise. Marinate the beef overnight in spices and mayonnaise.

2. Heat the Olive oil in a frying pan or wok and fry the spiralized cabbage for around 15 minutes until soft, then stew with the lid closed for around 15 minutes until the liquid is absorbed.

3. Grill the beef until golden brown and crispy. Spoon the soy sauce over the grilled beef. Then spoon the spiralized cabbage.

4. Sprinkle the salt and pepper and pour the freshly squeezed lemon juice over the spiralized cabbage and grilled beef and you are free to serve the grilled meat. Remember that this dish should be served warm.

Nutritional Information:

Calories: 326; Total fat: 67 oz; Total carbohydrates: 80 oz; Protein: 44 oz

Spiralized Potatoes and Grilled Beef in Garlic Mayonnaise

Prep Time: 20 min. | Cooking Time: 40-50 min. | Servings: 5

Ingredients:

25 oz beef, cubed

10 potatoes, peeled and spiralized

5 cups of garlic mayonnaise

5 tablespoons Olive oil

2 tablespoons soy sauce

5 tablespoons freshly squeezed lemon juice

1 teaspoon black pepper

3 tablespoons powdered garlic

½ teaspoon nutmeg

salt and pepper

How to Prepare:

1. In a bowl, combine powdered garlic, pepper, nutmeg, garlic mayonnaise and some salt. Season the beef with the salt and pepper, and toss in the powdered garlic, nutmeg and garlic mayonnaise. Marinate the beef overnight in spices and mayonnaise.

2. Heat the Olive oil in a frying pan or wok and fry the spiralized potatoes for around 15 minutes until soft, then stew with the lid closed for around 15 minutes.

3. Grill the beef until golden brown and crispy. Spoon the soy sauce over the grilled beef. Then add the spiralized potatoes.

4. Sprinkle the salt and pepper and pour the freshly squeezed lemon juice over the spiralized potatoes and grilled beef and you are free to serve the grilled meat with potatoes. Remember that this dish should be served warm.

Nutritional Information:

Calories: 356; Total fat: 69 oz; Total carbohydrates: 84 oz; Protein: 46 oz

Pork in Wine with Spiralized Squash and Cashews

Prep Time: 20 min. | Cooking Time: 40-50 min. | Servings: 5

Ingredients:

25 oz pork, cubed

1 squash, peeled and spiralized

3 glasses of wine

2 cups of cashews

5 tablespoons Olive oil

2 tablespoons soy sauce

5 tablespoons lime juice

1 teaspoon powdered chili pepper

2 tablespoons powdered garlic

½ teaspoon oregano

salt and pepper

How to Prepare:

1. Preheat the oven to 250°-280° Fahrenheit and roast the cashews in the oven for around 10 minutes until lightly browned and crispy.

2. In a bowl, combine powdered chili pepper, powdered garlic, oregano, and some salt. Season the pork with the salt and pepper, and toss in the powdered garlic, oregano, and powdered chili pepper mix. Marinate the pork overnight in spices and white wine.

3. Heat the Olive oil in a frying pan or wok and fry the spiralized squash for around 5 minutes until soft, then stew with the lid closed for around 5 minutes until the liquid is absorbed.

4. Grill the pork until golden brown and crispy. Spoon the soy sauce over the grilled pork. Then spoon the spiralized squash and cashews on top.

5. Sprinkle the salt and pepper and pour the lime juice over the spiralized squash and grilled pork and you are free to serve the grilled meat. Remember that this dish should be served warm.

Nutritional Information:

Calories: 346; Total fat: 70 oz; Total carbohydrates: 89 oz; Protein: 53 oz

Turkey Breast in Garlic Mayonnaise with Peanuts and Spiralized Beets

Prep Time: 30 min. | Cooking Time: 50-60 min. | Servings: 4

Ingredients:

20 oz turkey breast, cubed

2 cups of peanuts

2 cups of garlic mayonnaise

5 beets, peeled and spiralized

2 onions, spiralized

4 tablespoons white flour

5 tablespoons Olive oil

4 tablespoons soy sauce

5 tablespoons freshly squeezed lemon juice

1 teaspoon powdered chili pepper

3 tablespoons powdered garlic

salt and pepper

How to Prepare:

1. Preheat the oven to 230°-260° Fahrenheit and roast the peanuts in the oven for around 10 minutes until lightly browned and crispy.

2. In a bowl, combine powdered chili pepper, powdered garlic, and some salt. Season the turkey cubes with the salt and pepper, and toss in the powdered garlic and powdered chili pepper mix. Spoon the garlic mayonnaise over the turkey and marinate the turkey overnight in spices and mayonnaise.

3. Heat the Olive oil in a frying pan or wok and fry the turkey cubes for around 20 minutes until soft. Preheat the oven to 290°-320° Fahrenheit, and bake the cubed turkey for around 30-40 minutes. Toss the spiralized beets and onions in the Olive oil and salt. 20 minutes before the turkey is ready mix in the spiralized beets, onions and white flour. Mix well and stew them with the turkey cubes for a further 20 minutes.

4. Combine the soy sauce with the peanuts and spoon over the spiralized beets and turkey cubes.

5. Sprinkle the salt and pepper and pour the freshly squeezed lemon juice over the spiralized beets and turkey cubes and you are free to serve the turkey breast in separate bowls.

Nutritional Information:

Calories: 301; Total fat: 53 oz; Total carbohydrates: 70 oz; Protein: 42 oz

Chicken Breast in Garlic Mayonnaise with Peanuts and Spiralized Beets

Prep Time: 30 min. | Cooking Time: 40-50 min. | Servings: 4

Ingredients:

20 oz chicken breast, cubed

2 cups of peanuts

2 cups of garlic mayonnaise

5 beets, peeled and spiralized

2 onions, spiralized

4 tablespoons white flour

5 tablespoons Olive oil

4 tablespoons soy sauce

5 tablespoons freshly squeezed lemon juice

1 teaspoon powdered chili pepper

3 tablespoons powdered garlic

salt and pepper

How to Prepare:

1. Preheat the oven to 230°-260° Fahrenheit and roast the peanuts in the oven for around 10 minutes until lightly browned and crispy.

2. In a bowl, combine powdered chili pepper, powdered garlic, and some salt. Season the chicken cubes with the salt and pepper, and toss in the powdered garlic and powdered chili pepper mix. Spoon the garlic mayonnaise over the chicken and marinate the chicken overnight in spices and mayonnaise.

3. Heat the Olive oil in a frying pan or wok and fry the chicken cubes for around 20 minutes until soft. Preheat the oven to 290°-320° Fahrenheit, and bake the cubed chicken for around 30-40 minutes. Toss the spiralized beets and onions in the Olive oil and salt. 20 minutes before the chicken is ready mix in the spiralized beets, onions and white flour. Mix well and stew them with the chicken cubes for a further 20 minutes.

4. Combine the soy sauce with the peanuts and spoon over the spiralized beets and chicken cubes.

5. Sprinkle the salt and pepper and pour the freshly squeezed lemon juice over the spiralized beets and chicken cubes and you are free to serve the chicken breast in separate bowls.

Nutritional Information:

Calories: 304; Total fat: 54 oz; Total carbohydrates: 73 oz; Protein: 43 oz

Spicy Pork in Mustard with Peanuts, Pumpkin and Spiralized Beets

Prep Time: 30 min. | Cooking Time: 50-60 min. | Servings: 4

Ingredients:

20 oz pork, cubed

2 cups of peanuts

2 cups of mustard

6 beets, peeled and spiralized

2 onions, spiralized

2 cups of pumpkin, peeled and cubed

4 tablespoons white flour

5 tablespoons Olive oil

4 tablespoons soy sauce

5 tablespoons freshly squeezed lemon juice

2 teaspoons powdered chili pepper

4 tablespoons powdered garlic

salt and pepper

How to Prepare:

1. Preheat the oven to 230°-260° Fahrenheit and roast the peanuts in the oven for around 10 minutes until lightly browned and crispy.

2. In a bowl, combine powdered chili pepper, powdered garlic, and some salt. Season the pork cubes with the salt and pepper, and toss in the powdered garlic and powdered chili pepper mix. Spoon the mustard over the pork and marinate the pork overnight in spices and mustard.

3. Heat the Olive oil in a frying pan or wok and fry the pork cubes for around 20 minutes until soft. Preheat the oven to 290°-320° Fahrenheit, and bake the cubed pork for around 40-50 minutes. Toss the cubed pumpkin, spiralized beets and onions in the Olive oil and salt. 20 minutes before the pork meat is ready, mix in the pumpkin, spiralized beets,

onions and white flour. Stew them with the pork cubes for a further 20 minutes.

4. Combine the soy sauce with the peanuts and spoon over the spiralized beets and pork cubes.

5. Sprinkle the salt and pepper and pour the freshly squeezed lemon juice over the spiralized beets and pork cubes and you are free to serve the pork meat in separate bowls.

Nutritional Information:

Calories: 358; Total fat: 74 oz; Total carbohydrates: 93 oz; Protein: 58 oz

Inspiralized Potatoes with Lamb and Beef in Beer

Prep Time: 20 min. | Cooking Time: 50-60 min. | Servings: 6

Ingredients:

15 oz lamb, cubed

15 oz beef, cubed

2 cups of beer

1 cup of macadamia nuts

20 potatoes, peeled and spiralized

5 tablespoons sunflower oil

5 tablespoons freshly squeezed lemon juice

2 teaspoons powdered red pepper

4 tablespoons powdered garlic

2 teaspoons nutmeg, ground

salt and pepper

How to Prepare:

1. Preheat the oven to 220°-250° Fahrenheit and roast the macadamia nuts in the oven for around 10 minutes until lightly browned and crispy. Grind them using a food processor.

2. In a bowl, combine black pepper, powdered red pepper, powdered garlic, nutmeg, and some salt. Season the beef and lamb cubes with the salt and pepper, and toss in the powdered garlic, powdered red pepper, and nutmeg mix. Set the meat aside and marinate overnight in spices and 2-3 cups of beer.

3. Next day, preheat the oven to 320°-360° Fahrenheit, and bake the cubed beef and lamb for around 50-60 minutes until golden brown and crispy. Toss the spiralized potatoes in the sunflower oil and salt. 20 minutes before the meat is ready, open the oven and mix in the spiralized potatoes.

4. Spoon the macadamia over the spiralized potatoes and baked beef and lamb chunks.

5. Sprinkle the salt and pepper and pour the freshly squeezed lemon juice over the beef and lamb cubes. Now you are free to serve the spiralized potatoes with beef and lamb in separate plates. Serve this dish with the beer or glass of wine. Remember that this dish should be served warm.

Nutritional Information:

Calories: 494; Total fat: 86 oz; Total carbohydrates: 147 oz; Protein: 77 oz

Spiralized Zucchini with Turkey and Chicken in Beer

Prep Time: 20 min. | Cooking Time: 50-60 min. | Servings: 6

Ingredients:

15 oz turkey, cubed

15 oz chicken, cubed

2 cups of beer

1 cup of peanuts

1 zucchini, peeled and spiralized

3 carrots, peeled and spiralized

2 onions, peeled and spiralized

5 tablespoons Olive oil

5 tablespoons freshly squeezed orange juice

2 teaspoons powdered red pepper

4 tablespoons powdered garlic

2 teaspoons nutmeg, ground

salt and pepper

How to Prepare:

1. Preheat the oven to 220°-250° Fahrenheit and roast the peanuts in the oven for around 10 minutes until lightly browned and crispy. Grind them using a food processor.

2. In a bowl, combine black pepper, powdered red pepper, powdered garlic, nutmeg, and some salt. Season the turkey and chicken cubes with the salt and pepper, and toss in the powdered garlic, powdered red pepper, and nutmeg mix. Set the meat aside and marinate for at least 5 hours in spices and 2-3 cups of beer.

3. Next day, preheat the oven to 320°-360° Fahrenheit, and bake the cubed turkey and chicken for around 50-60 minutes until golden brown and crispy. Toss the spiralized zucchini, carrots and onions in the Olive oil and salt. 20 minutes before the turkey meat is ready, open the oven and mix in the spiralized vegetables.

4. Spoon the peanuts over the spiralized vegetables, baked turkey and chicken chunks.

5. Sprinkle the salt and pepper and pour the freshly squeezed orange juice over the turkey and chicken cubes. Now you are free to serve the spiralized vegetables with turkey and chicken in separate plates. Serve this dish with the glass of wine. Remember that this dish should be served warm.

Nutritional Information:

Calories: 394; Total fat: 64 oz; Total carbohydrates: 83 oz; Protein: 54 oz

Conclusion

Thank you for buying this spiralizer cookbook. I hope this was able to help you prepare tasty spiralizer recipes and eat healthier. This fourth spiralizer recipe book includes various spiralizer recipes with fish and meat. You can prepare these recipes for yourself, your friends or your family. **Thank you** and I hope you have enjoyed this.

If you've enjoyed this cookbook, I'd greatly appreciate if you could leave an honest opinion on Amazon.

Your opinions are very important to us authors, and it only takes a minute for you to post or contact me directly.

Your direct feedback could be used to help other readers to discover the advantages of spiralizer recipes!

If you have anything you want me to know, any questions, suggestions or feedback, please don't hesitate to contact me directly, through my Facebook page or email: ***books777@gmx.com***

If you have success story, please send it to me! I'm always happy to hear about my reader's success!

Thank you again and I hope you have enjoyed spiralizer cookbook.

Recipe Index

Apricots (14) Beef (24, 26, 29, 73, 76, 78, 91) Beer (29, 31, 33, 91, 93,) Cabbage (22, 33, 36, 76) Carrots (11, 20, 24, 41, 59) Cashews (36, 80) Celery (17, 61) Chicken (41, 68, 85, 93) Lamb (43, 45, 61, 91) Mayonnaise (43, 47, 50, 56, 59, 61, 71, 73, 76, 78, 82, 85) Milk (24, 26) Onions (22, 43, 45) Oranges (66, 68) Peanuts (26, 31, 33, 50, 59, 73, 82, 85, 88) Pineapple (11, 14, 17, 66, 68) Plums (20, 22) Pork (31, 33, 71, 80, 88) Potatoes (17, 29, 38, 41, 78, 91) Pumpkin (88) Raisins (11) Shrimps (11, 14, 17, 20, 22, 64, 66) Tuna (50, 53, 56) Turkey (36, 38, 82, 93) Walnuts (24, 29, 56) Zucchini (14, 26, 38, 47, 50, 56, 61, 64, 93)

Printed in Great Britain
by Amazon